This book is a tool to improve the way you feel about yourself.

I am using the power of our emotions to change the limiting beliefs that we have.

I researched how to be happy for many years before I stumbled upon this technique.

I used it on myself first and when I felt the positive change in me I shared the process with my daughter.

My goal is to share this technique to the kids around the world and make them feel happier.

Would you help me spread the knowledge by sharing this book with your friends and family?

Thank you!

Written by Angie Vezina

Illustrated by Jolie Hamm

Happy's Secret

I want to give a special thanks to Craig Sigl who taught me how to use my emotions in order to change my beliefs.

I am so grateful to have met Julie Francis who on top of being an awesome dermatologist, encouraged me to do something to help the kids.

Thanks to my daughter who opened my eyes and showed me that the teaching of this book is a blessing and should be shared.

Thanks to all of you for taking the time to read and use this book .
You are the best!

Written by Angie Vezina
Illustrated by Jolie Hamm

4

Once upon a time there was a boy named Max and a girl named Maya. They lived in a lovely little house on the top of a mountain surrounded by woods. Max was 7 years old, had crazy curly brown hair, and his eyes were the color of the sky. He was a dreamer and always imagined the most wonderful events and stories to tell his friends. Maya was 11 years old and very mature for her age. She had a very logical mind and would always be on time and prepared. She had lovely silky blond hair with deep brown eyes. They were brother and sister. You should see them, quite a happy pair always playing together and having fun.

One sunny summer day, they were outside playing and having so much fun that they did not notice the time flying by. Oh, oh! they were late for dinner. "Run! run!" said Maya, when she realized it was late. They ran full speed and arrived out of breath. "Phew! phew!" Maya opened the door as slowly as she could in order to make as little noise as possible. Max hid behind his big sister. The door squeaked. "Oh no!" Maya whispered, "We are going to get caught." Mother and father were sitting at the dinner table waiting for them. They did not look happy at all! The kids stared at their shoes as they went to sit at the table. Mom and dad were frowning.

Mom said in a stern voice: "Kids, you know we expect you to come home for dinner on time right?"

"Yes," Max and Maya said in duo.

"We did not see the time go by," said Maya.

"That is right," said Max.

"Well, try to be more careful next time, Dad and I worry about you, especially since we live in the woods."

The kids said, "sorry" in sad voices.

"On a better note," dad said, "you get to go visit with Aunt Stella for the weekend. Your mom and I have an important meeting to go too and we can't take you with us." "Oh!" said the kids. Max said, "the tornado" under his voice, and Maya giggled. Mom said, with a question mark in her voice, "what?" "Nothing," said the kids. You know, Aunt Tornado Oops I mean Aunt Stella was quite a character. She could be as sweet as honey one minute and the next, she could be as unpredictable as a tornado. Unpredictable means you don't know what is going to happen next. Uncle was the funny type, but they had twins that were quite the machiavellian pair. That big word means that they always came up with the most horrific plans to make them feel sad and guilty. Hang on, you will see what I mean later. Now let's go back to our story.

The kids finished eating dinner quietly, thinking about what was coming up in a near future. When they were done taking care of the dishes, the kids ran to their tree house. Maya was the first one up. When Max peeked his head through the opening he saw Maya sitting on the floor with her mouth open. There, was a creature sitting in the corner of the tree house looking at them. It had multi-colored, glowing, fluffy fur and big smiley eyes. Wow! they blinked their eyes at what they saw. They were astonished to see this strange, cuddly-looking creature and even more so when it started talking.

"Hi kids! my name is Happy!"
Maya and Max did not respond.
Happy said, "You look like you need a bit of cheering up."

The kids look down without saying anything, but thought about next weekend and the fact that Mom and dad were disappointed at them earlier.

Happy said, "I have a secret that I would love to share with you. It will make you feel better. Want to hear about it?"

The kids nodded.

Happy said, "When you feel sad or guilty you need to repeat the following magic words: I am worth it. I forgive myself. I can do it. I love myself. Repeat all of those magic words or select a few, it is up to you."

"Would you like to try it?"

You know, the kids did not really believe that this would make them feel any better but because they were polite, they said, "Sure, we shall try it."

Happy said: "Which magic words did you choose?"
Max said, "I chose" I forgive myself.
Maya said, "I chose" I am worth it.

"Cool!" said Happy. "Now, next time you feel sad or guilty or... Just tell yourself those magic words and you will feel happier. Repeat those words every time the sad, guilty feelings return."

You know there are different reasons why grown ups, siblings and friends are sometimes mean to you, it happens, nothing is perfect. What matters is that it does not affect you and that you are able to let it go and be happy.

Max and Maya looked at each other skeptically. That means they were not sure if this would really work.

Happy was tearing up with joy at the idea that his secret would be used and would change the lives of those kids.They now had a trick to change the way they felt about themselves.

Before he left he told the kids.

"If you need help, just say my name three times in a row. Just like this: 'Happy! Happy! Happy!' and I will appear to you."

"Ok," said the kids.

Pouf! in a rainbow of light he was transformed into millions of colorful tiny stars and floated through the window.

"Wow," said Maya.

"I am not sure if I am dreaming," said Max.

"What do you think about what just happened?" said Maya.

"Well I am willing to give it a try," said Max.

"Ok," said Maya, "but I don't think it will work."

"Why not!" said Max.

"It sounds too easy," said Maya

"Look at the sunset," said Max.

"It is beautiful," said Maya, "but it makes me think that it is time for us to go home."

That night they prepared for bed time and fell asleep thinking about the strange encounter they had that day.

12

Friday came way too quickly because this was the weekend they were going to go to see the evil twins.

After school on Friday both kids were playing together outside, when their parents told them to come in and finish packing up because they had to leave soon.

When they arrived at their Aunt's house, the whole family was outside enjoying a late dinner. The twins were torturing a poor frog who had the bad luck to be in their path.

Aunt Stella said, "Come and join us for dinner." Mom said, "We would love too but we really need to go if we want to be on time for our conference." She kissed Max and Maya on their foreheads, gave them a big hug, and left with dad in a hurry.

"Bye," said the kids with a sad tone. Aunt Stella said, "Oh, come on kids this will be fun. Nick and Pick have been anxious to see you and play with you both." You know the kids did not feel the same way at all. They knew how mean those two could be, not to say how much of a bad temper their aunt could be in. Oh well! it is only for two days but time will go soooo slowwww, they were thinking. You know how when you are not enjoying yourself time seem to go super slow.

"Lets go play in the wine cellar," said Nick. "Cool," said the others. "What is a wine cellar?" asked Max. "It is where you make and store wine," said Maya. "Wooo!!!! That sounds cool," said Max.

Nick and Pick started running, followed by Max and Maya. They soon got to the wine cellar door. It looked like one of those tornado hide out. There, were two doors that needed to be open and a staircase that lead to the basement. Nick opened the door and told Max and Maya: "Since you are our guests you should have the privilege of going first." He winked at his brother. "Ok," said Max. Maya was a bit scared, but she did not want her cousins to think that she was afraid, so she followed Max. It was dark in there. The steps were made of woods. Brrr, the cellar was scary and cold even on this hot summer night. When they reached the bottom of the stairs they heard a big clunk. "Oh no! what was that?" they said in unison. (unison means together) They turned around and realized that the evil twins had closed the doors of the cellar and locked them in. Maya and Max screamed, "let us out! let us out!" But the evil twins were laughing and enjoying their prank way too much to let it end so quickly. Max and Maya climbed back up the stairs and started to pound on the door while screaming and crying for their cousins to let them out.

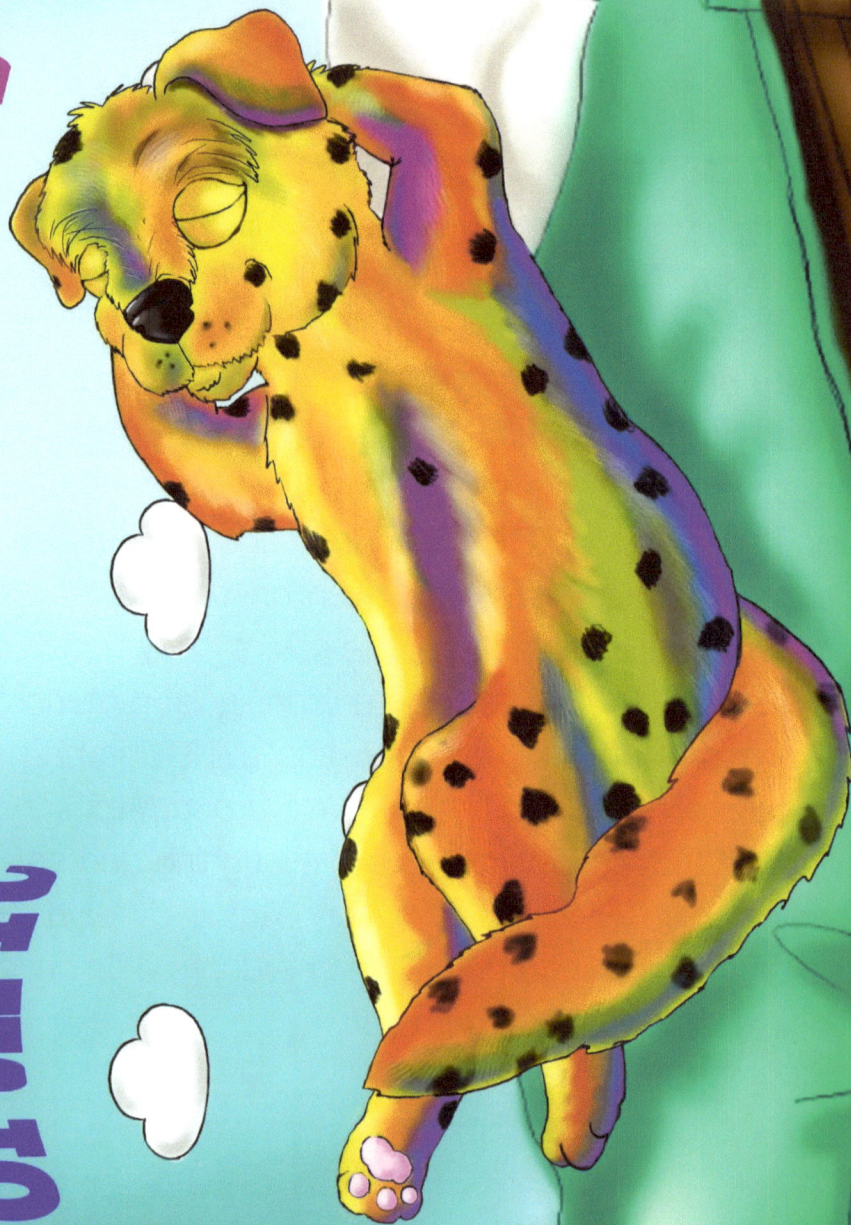

I can do this

I forgive myself

I am worth it

worth it

16

Fortunately, their uncle was passing by and saw the twins laughing while rolling on the ground. "Hey, what is so funny?" said Pepper. "Nothing," said the twins. But there it was: the faint yelling of Max and Maya. Pepper looked at the cellar doors that were locked from the outside and quickly opened them. Maya and Max jumped out and Pepper hugged them real hard.

Uncle turn his gaze toward his sons and told them, "Kids, go to your room. You are grounded for the rest of the evening. We will talk later." The evil twins were no longer laughing, they went home dragging their feet. Pepper told Max and Maya, "I am so sorry. I will talk to them so they don't do that again."

Once in their bedroom Maya said to Max, "I can't believe they did that to us." "I agree," said Max, "I am so angry at them I would like to kick them." "Me too," said Maya. "I am super sad and can't wait to go back home." But then a twinkle appeared in Max's eye. He said, "Why don't we try Happy's secret?" "Sure", said Maya. She closed her eyes and repeated in her head I am worth it. Max did the same thing and told himself I forgive myself. After a few minutes of repeating those words. They looked at each other and said,"Wow, it worked! I feel great!" "I wonder if it works all the time," said Maya. "I bet it does," said Max, excitedly. "I wonder what Happy is doing right now," said Maya. Look at the picture to see what Happy is doing.

The next day was a stormy day. The wind was blowing and you could hear the thunder. "What is all that scary noise?" said Max and Maya. On their side of the mountain, they barely ever have thunder and lightning. In fact, the kids had never experienced it until now.

Aunt Stella said, "You can't tell me that you don't know what thunder is. How old are you again? Five?" The twins started making fun of them, "Look at them! They're scared of a little storm. What a bunch of babies".

At that moment, they felt so ashamed but then, Max said to Maya, "think about Happy". Maya looked at him and a smile appeared on her face. They both thought about Happy and repeated to themselves, "I love myself." In a matter of minutes they felt brand new and they were on top of the world. The cousins looked at each other wondering why they were so happy, especially after they made fun of them. You know, in life most kids who try to make you feel bad about yourself do that because they personally don't feel so good about themselves so they want you to feel the same way.

The twins said, "Why are you so happy? "Max and Maya looked at each other and said, "We have a secret." "Ohhh, what is it?" the boys said. "Before we tell, you need to take us to your fortress." said Maya "Ok," said the twins.

Into the forest they went. After a while Pick said, "Here it is." He pulled a few branches aside and there it was, a beautiful waterfall. "Wow!" said Maya and Max. "This is our most secret place," said the twins, "now it is your turn, tell us your secret."

Maya and Max said, "Happy, Happy, Happy!" Pouf, out of nowhere, Happy appeared. "Wow," said the twins. "What can I do to help you on this lovely day? I heard my name and saw your faces." said Happy.

"Well you said we could call you if we needed help," said Max. "That is true," said Happy. "We figured that our cousins must be pretty insecure if they need to put us down in front of others." said Maya. "You are right." said Happy. "Would you tell them what you taught us?" said Max. "You bet. Here is what I teach the kids around the world. It is very simple and yet very powerful. When you feel sad close your eyes and tell yourself: I am worth it, I love myself, I forgive myself. Now do this every time you feel insecure or guilty or...". Said Happy.

"You are right," said Nick, "that is too simple." "And yet," said Happy, "did you see Max and Maya after they did this when you were making fun of them?" "Yep!" said Nick. "You saw enough of a difference to show them your secret place, right?" said Happy. "I see your point," said Nick. "You now know the secret of happiness. I need to go and help other kids learn this secret." said Happy. "Bye," said the kids. Pouf, in a rainbow of tiny stars, Happy disappeared in the sky.

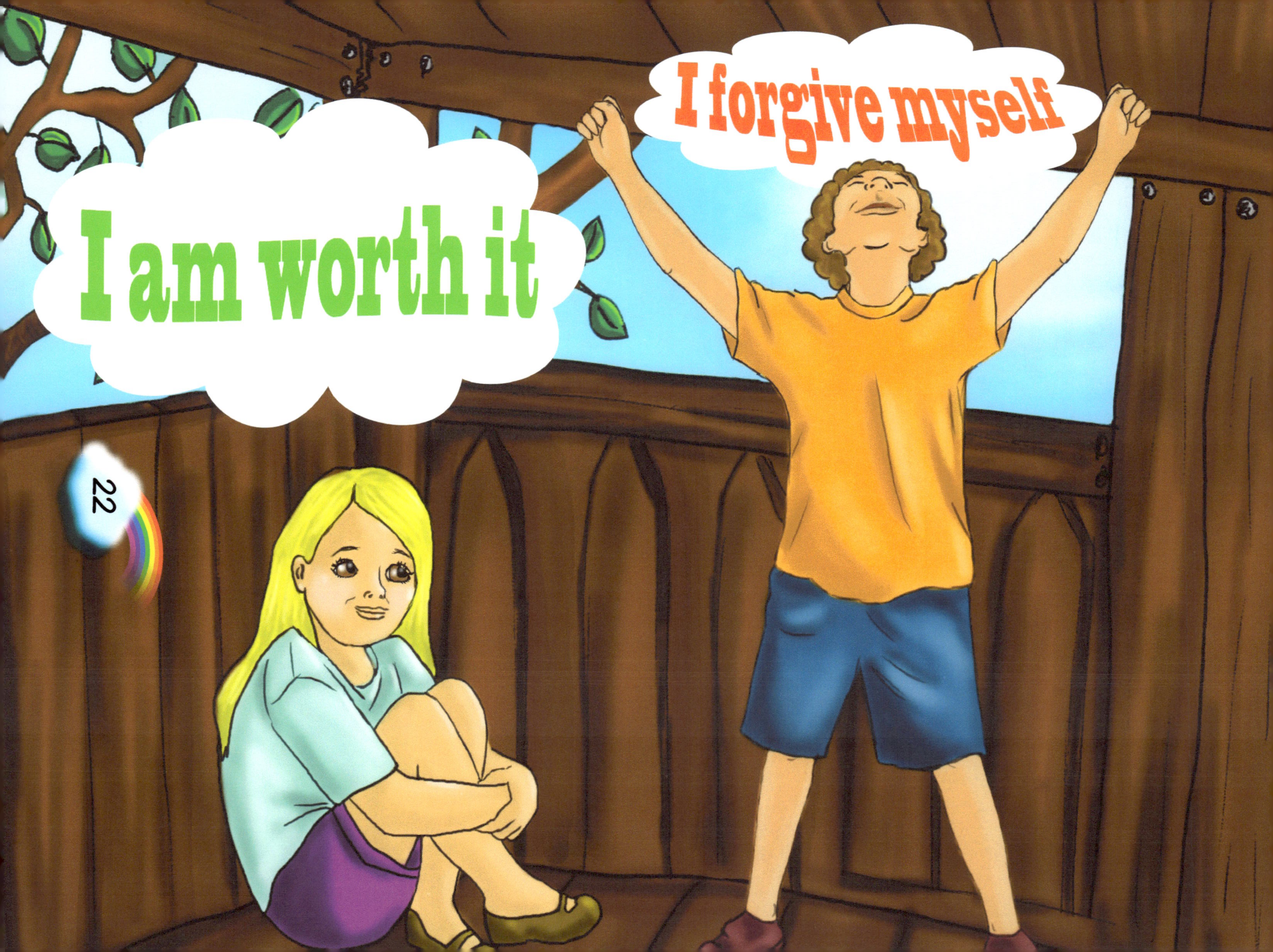
I am worth it
I forgive myself

Nick and Pick looked at Max and Maya who had big grins on their faces and said, "We are sorry we made you feel sad and ashamed. "We forgive you," said Maya and Max. "Will you be using Happy's secret?" "Sure," said Nick "I will, too" said Pick. You know, sometimes aunt Stormy was a bit rough and made them feel pretty bad, which is why they would in turn take revenge against their friends and cousins.

Sunday came very quickly. It was a sunny day with a few white clouds. The kids heard the bell telling them breakfast was ready. They rushed down to the kitchen where an awesome breakfast was waiting for them. Later on that day when they got back home Max said to Maya, "Want to go to the tree house?" "Sure," said Maya.

Max climbed up first this time and looked around, but Happy was not there. Then it was Maya's turn and Max said to her, "he is not here."

"Well," Maya said, "he did help us, right?"

"Right," said Max. So we don't really need him anymore for now, right?" "Right," said Max.

They both looked at each other smiled and started humming the following song.

When I feel sad, when I feel mad, I start singing

I can do it, I forgive myself, I am worth it

Wow! what a change, life is good, I can feel it.

The end!

www.ingramcontent.com/pod-product-compliance
Lightning Source LLC
LaVergne TN
LVHW072110070426
835509LV00002B/108